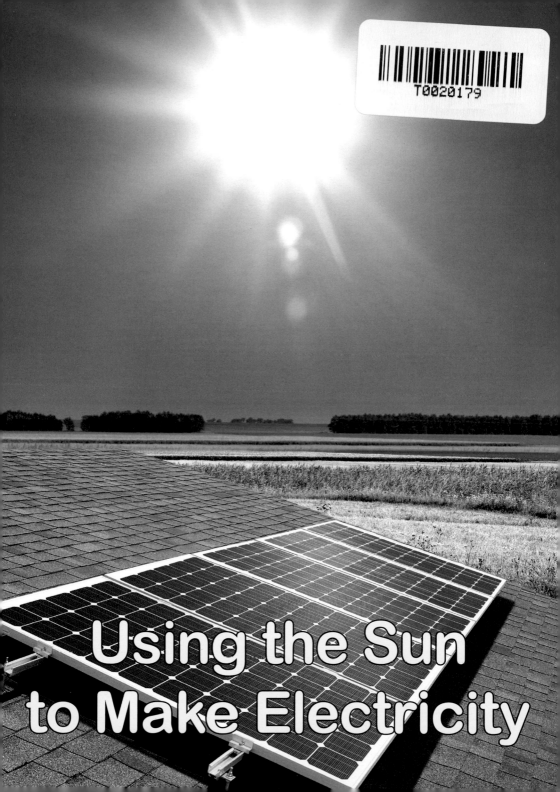

Using the Sun
to Make Electricity

The sun is hot.

The sun is on my face.

5

The sun is on my shirt.

Look at this.

The sun is on this too.

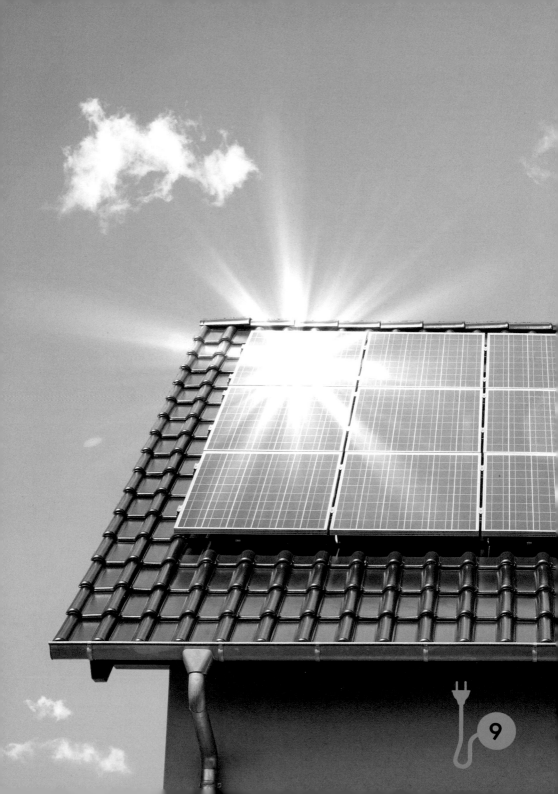

9

The sun will **shine.**

The sun will make electricity.

The electricity will make my **keyboard** go.
The electricity will make my iPad go.

The sun will shine on and on and on.

Glossary

keyboard

shine